THE BEST ME! ENVIRONMENT

Join Our Earth Club!

by
Kimmie Auntie

Illustrations by
Ayeshe Sadr & Ishaan Dasgupta

another title brought to you from
the BEST ME series

SCHOLASTIC
New York Toronto London Auckland
Sydney New Delhi Hong Kong

To my Dad, who shares his
love of Earth with us

Published by Scholastic India Pvt. Ltd.
A subsidiary of Scholastic Inc., New York, 10012 (USA).
Publishers since 1920, with international operations in Canada, Australia, New Zealand, the United Kingdom, India, and Hong Kong.

For information regarding permission, write to:
Scholastic India Pvt. Ltd.
A-27, Ground Floor, Sigma Centre
Infocity-1, Sector 34, Gurgaon 122001 (India)

First edition : December 2016

This edition : October 2022

ISBN-13: 978-93-8610-675-9

Printed by Sterling Graphics Pvt. Ltd., Manesar

Dear friend,

The thing is—we only got one earth to share. You may have a few pairs of shoes and a few more toys and I hope a lot of books—but we all only have one earth. One. That's it. And while it is only one, we're lucky, it is a magnificent ONE! Our earth has rolling gold green hills to love, and sparkly rivers to play in, and tangerine sands to dance in. Our earth is amazing.

But, we need to learn to share the earth with everyone and everything. Sharing is good. So, please, do your part. Learn how to be a good friend with the earth.

Join Our Earth Club!

Truly,
Kimmie Auntie

Sargam busted through the door,

Max came **bounding**, twirling, jumping, leaping and finally **crashed** into his mother.

He scrambled up and struck a pose, "Guess who I am?"

Mom looked Max over...
All of Max's 97 centimetres were grey!

His legs were covered with grey pants. His belly was covered with his grey t-shirt. Even his hands were stuffed inside grey socks. Silly swim goggles were strapped across his face.

What was this?

His bare feet stuck out below and a red cape stuck out behind. His hair stuck up all over—but that was normal.

Mom suggested, "Uh, you are an elephant going for a swim?"

Max giggled. "Noooo!"

"You are a zoo keeper"

"Ha. NO!" Max snorted.

"A bus driver?"

Max shook his head.

"An astronaut?"

"Nope."

Mom whispered, "I think I need a hint..."

Max bounced over to the gate. He stopped suddenly with his hands on his hips.

"I am a SUPERHERO GATE!"

He looked very brave with his hands on his hips.

Mom's forehead crinkled. "I have never heard of a SUPERHERO GATE..." she puzzled.

Max threw up his hands. "**Moooom!** I just invented it. You know, kids sometimes have a hard time choosing to be healthy—so I will help."

LET'S ALL BE HEALTHY!

Mom smiled. She knew Max had a hard time being healthy *all* the time. "Ok. But how does a SUPERHERO GATE help kids be healthy?"

"I figured it out.

Being healthy mostly means good things IN and bad things OUT. But sometimes that is tricky. I, the SUPERHERO GATE, can help kids keep things in the right place!"

Mom was curious. "What things should be kept in the right place?"

"Germs!"
he cried.

"Every day I brush my teeth and take a bath. I wash my hands before I eat and I don't use the glass or fork of a friend who is sick. I keep germs OUT." With his superhero arms wide, he spun to chase the germs away.

Max came to a stop with a grin, "You know I love toffees? And cold drinks?" Oh yes, Mom knew.

"To be healthy I should only eat a little bit of snack foods. I keep junk food OUT ... mostly."

Mom hugged him. "Mostly is ok."

With a superhero giant puff of air, Max blew away the JUNKs. "I am also going to keep junk OUT of my head!"

Max stopped long enough to nod wisely, "Yup, I don't want my head polluted with abuse words or mean thoughts. I won't call my sisters names ... even just to myself. And I will even watch less TV ... I want a healthy head too!"

Mom's eyebrows popped up. "You are a SUPERHERO GATE!"

"Healthy kids need to know all the things to keep *IN!*" exclaimed Max.

"Like what?" asked his mom.

"Water!" Max cried with a bounce. "Every day I should exercise and drink water. Healthy means exercise and water *IN!*"

Mom cheered.

Max made a face. “But I don’t like vegetables...”

Mom considered for a moment. “Well, a SUPERHERO GATE would need to eat vegetables to be strong.” Max shrugged his shoulders. He guessed he would have to.

Mom added, "Water and vegetables are important things to keep *IN* your body. But what things can you keep *IN* for a healthy mind and heart?"

Max thought about it...

Looking up from her book, Vidya flipped her hair back. "Didi, why are you so flustered?!"

(Vidya loves using big words.)

"I've just been exploring—"
DO YOU KNOW HOW AWESOME EARTH IS?

"Yes!" whooped Max.

Sargam chuckled, "You're little, Max.
What do you know?"

"I know that hummingbirds can fly backwards," he spouted as he zoomed in reverse.

"And butterflies taste with their feet."

Sargam hopped in, "Yes, and elephants can smell water three miles away! Pigs understand each other's grunts—they can even say, 'I'm hungry!' And when peacocks gather in a group, it's called a party!"

"Wow! A peacock party!" gushed Vidya.

"We need to start an Earth Club,"
Sargam declared with a determined thump.
"Everyone has to do their part!"

Vidya yelped, "But we're just kids!"

"Exactly! We can do a lot!"
assured Max with a superhero twirl.
"We can save the whole earth!"

Smiling, Sargam plopped on her thinking cap and pulled out a list. "Max, I think there's a lot we can do right here.

Let's go, Earth Club!"

Vidya cheered.
She always cheers.

Max bounced.
He always bounces.

Flipping off the AC switch, Sargam started. "I bet we could use fans a lot of the time—that saves energy! And make sure the TV is always turned off."

Vidya cheered, "We could use sunlight rather than tube lights too!"

Max slammed the light switch off with a superhero spin. "What else?"

Sargam checked her list,
"We never litter ...
but we could also recycle
our garbage. And maybe
give our used clothes and
books to others."

Vidya peered in the dustbin,

"Hey! What's this?"

Max trudged over.

"I guess I could fix my truck

rather than buying a new one."

Sargam added,
"I also learned
we should buy
rechargeable
batteries
for our toys.
Less waste!"

Max whooped,
"Superheroes
never waste!"

Vidya cheered.
"Earth Club members—
let's go scout!"

First, they traipsed to the bathroom ... Uh-oh.
The faucet was dripping! Vidya cranked it shut.

"We also have to turn off the tap when we brush our teeth!"

"Good idea, Vids!" bounced Max.

Next, the Earth Club investigated the kitchen.
Max got distracted, "How about a snack?"

Sargam suggested, "I learned it takes a lot of energy to produce meat.
Let's eat more veg food!"

Max high-fived Sargam—
"I like animals alive!"

"I can pack my tiffin in a metal box—plastic ones break too easily," added Vidya. "And I can give my leftovers to a cow."

"Remember—don't give cows plastic bags!" reminded Sargam, "Cows eat plastic bags, get sick and can even die."

Max nodded. "I like happy cows!"

Last they explored out of doors...

"Maybe we should play outside more," Sargam marvelled, "it's nice out here!"

Spotting a plastic bag, Max swooped to pick it up. "We can keep it nice too!"

Vidya glanced around, "Our yard sure could use a shady tree ... maybe that could be my birthday present?"

They all flopped down and
Sargam drafted the Earth Club Pledge.

EARTH CLUB PLEDGE

I, Sargam, pledge to love Mother Earth and all her animals and even her insects and maybe even the frogs and to share the Earth properly....

Signed,
with a pinky promise.

"I can do it!" promised Vidya.

"We need a secret handshake," whispered Max.

(Every club needs a secret handshake.)

Vidya coloured some
Earth Club badges.

"Hey, let's invite our
friends to join ..."

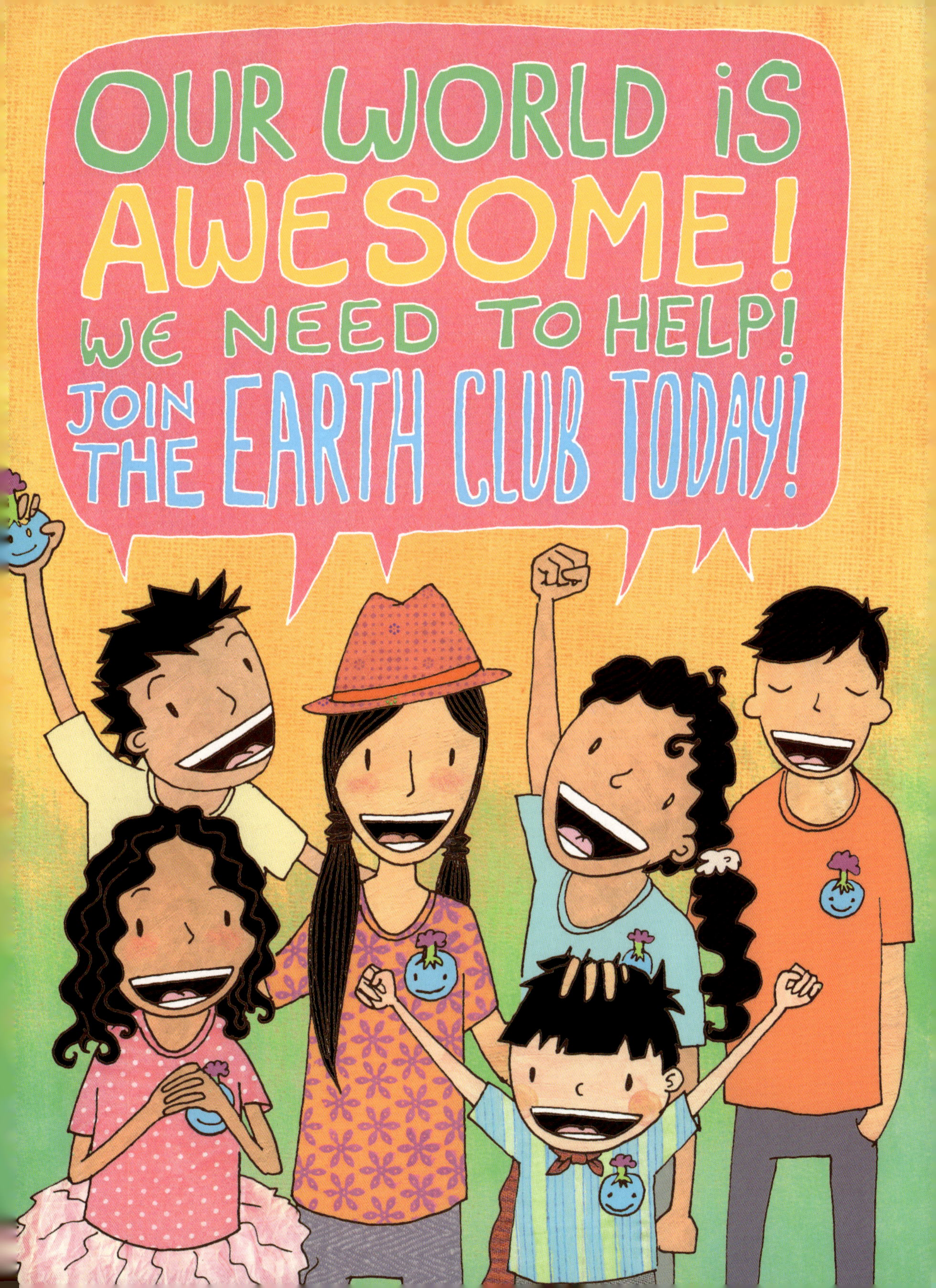
OUR WORLD IS AWESOME!
WE NEED TO HELP!
JOIN THE EARTH CLUB TODAY!

Discussion Questions for Parents and Teachers:

- What does conserve mean?
- Why should we conserve the environment?
- What do we already do?
- What can we do better?

(There are environmental behaviours an adult knows that you can share with a kid—such as CFL light bulbs or buying organic or not littering.)

Activities:

1. Take the kids out to enjoy nature—they need to love it before they will want to conserve it!

2. Have an "experience" birthday party. Rather than having your child (or you!) receive a lot of things that will break quickly or go straight to the gift cupboard, throw a "no gifts" party and take everyone for an adventure!

3. Go on YouTube and watch 'The Story of Stuff' with your kids. If you're inspired, you can also watch the 'Story of Solutions'. Talk to your kids about what this means.

*Parenting Tip:
What you do, your kids will learn!

And when you need to encourage them a little, "Hey, who's in the Earth Club?" will help remind them to not litter or to turn off the tap.